Daily Inspirations
for Spiritual Growth

by Brei Carter

Author photograph by

John Fidele

Art direction by

John Elkins
Creative

johnelkinscreative.com

Daily Inspirations for Spiritual Growth

by Brei Carter

ISBN 978-0-578-06167-2

This book is dedicated to God who is the head of my life, for without Him, this book would not have been possible.

To my parents Rev and Mrs John Griggs who instilled in me the value of prayer, praise and worship. To look to God first always and then to look inside myself.

To my family and closest and dearest friends who encouraged me to continue on my journey and allowed me to encourage them along their path in their daily walk on life.

Many Blessings to all who read this and may it add additional comfort to you daily.

INDEX

26. Others want what you have.

27. Do you know what I know?

28. Got me going in circles!

29. Do you BLOG?

30. Let it go!

31. What's your worth?

32. When God has a plan....

33. It's time to take off the gloves.

34. Don't worry, be happy!

35. Do you remember or did you forget?

36. What do you do?

37. God wants more for you!

38. Do you remember the time?

39. Stop! Selah! Listen! Focus!

40. Make things happen.

41. It's not about you!

42. Make it plain!

43. What rules you?

44. It's another day's journey.

45. Watch out!

46. Time to be ye steadfast.

47. Believe!

48. Acceptable or not?

49. STAND!

50. You have the power!

51. What's going on?

52. Check yourself!

53. You can make it!

54. Do you worry?

55. Isn't he wonderful?

56. Who's in control?

57. Today is going to be a great day!

58. Don't stop, keep on going!

59. You really have the victory!

60. No matter where you are in life!

61. You are where you're supposed to be.

62. On your mark!

63. Knock! Knock!

64. Are you driving?

65. Amazing grace!

66. Do you ever wonder why?

67. Never forget!

68. Time to shine!

69. Get in the zone!

70. Release the knots and renew your mind!

71. Today is a new beginning, so embrace this moment with celebration!

72. Cherish the moment!

73. Showtime! Lights! Camera! Action?

74. Divine intervention!

75. Go deep!

76. We all wonder!

77. God has the final say so!

78. Live a life of no regret!

79. Time for a temperature check!

80. New chapter. Next book.

81. What are you wearing?

82. Process=smile & the world smiles with you! Frown & world ignores you!

83. Keep believing, keep hoping.

84. Stop! Look! Listen!

85. Let not your heart be troubled, God is with you ALWAYS!

86. Call now!

87. There's so much going on in the world today!

88. Do you know the answers?

89. Rejoice and be happy!

90. Oh how amazing it is to rise and see another day!

91. Love, mercy and grace: God's greatest gifts.

92. Clean house!

93. Driving?

94. It's time to take watch!

95. Life without limitations!

96. Don't let it get you down!

97. A year has passed you by.

98. It's time to release the fears deep within that cause you to be in bondage!

99. Sweet whispers and a gentle touch.

100. Let Him lead you!

Open up!

Open up! It's time to awaken your mind to fresh new possibilities. It's time to release those fears that hold you back. It's time to be open to all that God has for you! Why not move beyond, not giving your all at everything you do, because life can be as grand as you make it! Start today by looking inward. Open up and ask what you can do to make a difference! It's not so much what others can do for you. It's about *you*. It's about being true to who you are and who God has called you to be. Open up! Because when you don't, others lose. But remember you *do* miss out!

It's Simple!

The road gets tough and sometimes decisions are hard to make. Is the journey you're on pleasing you? Pleasing to the Lord? Are you tired? It's time to re-evaluate things. God says, "Come to me all those who are heavy laden and burdened and He will give you rest!" He will renew your strength. Seek ye first the kingdom of Heaven and all will be added unto you! So whatever road you take or decision you make, remember that God can make a way! It's simple! The journey you embark upon will be full of unexpected surprises and you can never prepare for them all. So stand tall and call on your Heavenly Father. He can make a way out of no way. Call on Jesus! It's simple!

Is it in Vain?

Is it in vain? Of course not! It's eternal gain! Is your living, giving or praying in vain? God says no! He desires more of you! He wants us to surrender all to Him. It's time to realize that you must not get weary in your well doing. You will be rewarded. He will give you double for your troubles. Give and it shall be given back to you. It is not in vain. Be the best that you can be! God is calling you and your good deeds are not in vain.

Just ask, He says...

He said, "You have not because you've asked not." But when you ask you must believe that you've already received the things you're asking for! First, ask God to create a clean spirit in you. Ask Him to cover you, protect and forgive you. You can have it all, but what profits a man to gain the whole world and lose His soul? Ask God to lead, guide and direct your path. Just ask and trust your Heavenly Father because you're gonna make it! Know that all things are possible to those that believe. So no matter what you're going through, know that *nothing* is too hard for God. Just ask. "Just ask," He says!

Shhhhh

"Shhhhh," says the teacher to the little child. Sound familiar? I'm sure growing up we've all heard that a time or two. It's time to quiet your mind and open your heart. Remember, God says that we must humble ourselves and come unto Him as little children. It's time to go back to the basics. He says, "Be still and know that I am God." Put your hope in the Lord. He can't fail you. As an adult we quite often want to analyze and rationalize things but God says to trust Him and lean not to your own understanding. When we put our true *hope* in God we are happy and open to endless possibilities. We praise God and surrender. We seek eternal life. So today close your mouth, quiet your mind and open your heart. Have faith, for faith is the substance of things hoped for and the evidence of the unseen.

What should I do?

What steps should I take? What move should I make? God, I need you now more than ever. Free me from the impure thoughts that enter my mind. I know God that you created Heaven and Earth and all there within. It is you that made me and not me myself. Some attack my character and some attack my integrity, but God I ask you to rescue me. Father you said in all my ways to acknowledge you and you would direct my path. You are my all, and I can't make it without you! Thank you for all you're doing, for all you've done and all that you plan to do. I celebrate you my Heavenly Father! Please tell me, what should I do?

Stop and think before you speak!

What are you saying on a daily basis? What are the words that come from your mouth? Do you mean what you say? Do you say what you mean? The words of your mouth and the meditation of your heart should be pleasing and acceptable to the Lord! The Lord is your rock and He is your redeemer. It is better to be thought a fool than to open your mouth and remove all doubt. Remember that life and death are in the power of the tongue, so carefully think and choose your words for they are powerful! Speak love, healing and blessings over your life and the lives of others. What you say matters! Stop and think before you speak!

Let's TALK! Make it a Priority!

TALK =

Teach others about Gods greatness.

Acknowledge that God can never fail.

Love always.

Keep the faith and believe!

Whatever priorities you make in your life will dictate your life, so choose carefully! There is more to life! Are you truly experiencing God's best? Where are you priorities and should you re-evaluate them? Take time to fulfill someone else's needs. We all have a part to play in this world. Are you playing yours? TALK = Top Priority.

You Can Do It!

You can do it! Yes, you can! Are you doing all that you can do and being all that you can be? Do you find reasons to make excuses and put things off for another day? Do you realize that tomorrow is not promised? Why put off 'til tomorrow what can be done today? Take a long hard look at what and who you have been putting off! Get it together! When I was a child I thought like a child and acted like a child, but now you are a man/woman so it's time to act, think and talk like it! Put away childish things and come into the fullness of your potential. It's not about being serious all the time, but it is about being mature and making mature decisions. Just as God wants us to mature in Him and learn and grow, we are to do the same things here on Earth. So I say you can do it. Yes, you can! It's time to close a chapter and start anew. It's time to take responsibility for your life. You can do all things through Christ who strengthens you! You can do it!

Make up your mind!

Whatever it is that's been weighing on your mind, seek God and He will show you what to do! If the Lord leads you there it can't be wrong! Remember though when you ask God, you must believe and not doubt. Anyone who doubts is like a wave in the sea, blown up and down by the wind. God wants you to stand and be strong. God wants you to have faith and show action, because faith without works is dead! Faith cometh by hearing and doing the word of God! If you don't stand for something you're likely to fall for anything. So take some quiet time and seek your Father and let Him lead, guide and direct you! A righteous man's steps are ordered by the Lord! Pray and ask your Father what you should do daily and in every aspect of your life. The time to make a decision is now, so make up your mind!

Realize that you are never alone!

Never Alone! Never Alone! Just know that you don't have to worry because you are never alone! God walks beside you every day, along the way, forever by your side. He said lo I am with you always. There's a blessed assurance in knowing that when God is on our side, that things will work out fine. He says for us to put our hope and trust in Him. We should not worry, but instead we must look up to the hills from whence cometh our help. Our help comes from the Lord! Just know that He is an on time God! He's always there. When you feel like He's not there and you don't feel His presence He's still there! Wait on the Lord and watch what you say. Life and death are in the power of the tongue. Your Father in Heaven has everything worked out and planned for you so continue pray without ceasing! Just know whatever you do, whatever you're going through, that you are never alone! To God be the glory always! Thank God Almighty you are never alone!

He said it!

"Be still and know that I am God!" What's on your mind? What consumes your thoughts? Turn it all over to God and let it go! If you worry, why pray? And if you pray, why worry? We should be anxious for nothing! Are you waiting on the Lord or are you in a hurry? Let God dictate your life and not man. He is the Great I Am and none are greater than Him! Encourage yourself daily, because society will put demands on your life if you keep the faith. Know that the Lord's goodness will prevail in your life. Smile today and count it all as joy as things comes your way today! You are more than a conqueror! Remember God says that nothing is too hard for Him, too big for Him or too small for Him! He can do all things but fail. So cast all your cares on Him for He cares for you! He is your shepherd and you shall not want! Read the word, He said it!

There's more than what meets the eye.

Life is multifaceted! There are so many undiscovered dimensions in our own lives. We should all take the time to reconnect with ourselves to see who we really are. It's amazing how God knows every hair on our head. He knows everything about us! He knew us when we were in our mother's womb. He knows everything about us, yet He still loves us in spite of our flaws and short comings. We don't have to hide from Him! God can create in us a pure heart, He can make us white as snow! Just ask! Jesus died on the cross for our salvation! Would you lay your life down for another? Look around, just look around because in the midst of whatever you're going through someone needs you! Maybe someone recently received bad news about a family member, a job or maybe the doctor gave them a bad report and the prognosis doesn't look good. Who are you and in what capacity can you help them? Maybe a kind word, or a listening ear? Maybe a smile or maybe a shoulder to cry on? Maybe a financial blessing or maybe just being there? I don't know for sure your mission or purpose, but I do know there's more to you! You are special. You are precious. You are wonderfully made, so let God use you. Don't put off tomorrow for what you can do today! Search yourself and study to show yourself approved by God! Remember there's many dimensions within waiting to be uncovered! People helping people! I know there's more than meets the eye.

Did you know?

Did you know that God *for* you is more than the world *against* you? Take the time to celebrate and praise the Lord for He is worthy! Do you ever think where you'd be without God? Keep in mind and never forget that it's not by your will and might, but His Power! He has all power in His hands. Sometimes we think we have all the answers and have it figured out, but we must realize that it's God's grace and mercy that saved us! He won't let you stumble and fall or your foot to be removed. He's a just, loving and compassionate God. He's your Heavenly Father, and He's with you at all times. When is the last time you called on Him? I think it's time to call Him up and tell Him what you wanted and what you need. Remember that God's favor is more than anything you could accomplish on your own. It opens doors that no man can shut, and puts you at the right place at the right time. It places you ahead of all that tries to hinder.

FAVOR =

Future

Advancing

Victory

Opportunities

Released

Did you know FAVOR ain't always fair? Did you know?

PRAY! Please pray.

Release the authority! You need to release the authority that God has given you! Do you know your worth? Speak blessings over your life. You are what you say you are and you can have whatever you say! As long as you quite believe it in your heart and doubt not and it's the will of God! Don't be disappointed when a situation hasn't quite gone as you thought or planned, just know that your Heavenly Father has something else better for you. Desire to have God's will for your life because it supersedes what you think is best for you. God knows what's best for you! Do you? Release the authority that God has given you. God has given you the power and it's time to exercise your faith. You can move mountains. You can have good health, houses and land, great jobs and peace in your life. You can be healthy, wealthy and wise. Today seek God! Ask for wisdom, and in all thy getting, get an understanding! It's time to understand your authority and not underestimate it! Please pray. Release the authority!

When the lights go out, who do you call?

Whoever you decide to call, think of calling Jesus! When you call on Jesus, all things are possible! Late in the midnight hour while your mind is wandering, God has already turned things around. Even if you don't understand, know that it will be in your favor! God is good, so let Him know that He's worthy in your life and you truly love Him. When the lights go out and you can't sleep and you feel like you're alone, your body aches and within you're seeking peace. You really want to talk and need to talk. Why not call on your Heavenly Father? God gives you peace that no man can take away. So when people walk out of your life, and it's time to leave that job or it ends or you don't know where the money is coming from, don't worry! Call on God! Believe it in your heart and doubt not in your mind. Ask, believing that you have already received! He's able! So call on the Lord! When the lights go out, just know that you can *always* call on God.

Is it worth it?

It has not been in vain! I know it seems like things sometime remain the same, but I'm here to tell you that it has not been in vain! Never get weary in well-doing, for the Lord says your reward will be great! The least among you will be the greatest! Hold on, breakthrough won't be denied and it won't be delayed any longer. Guard your thoughts and watch the words that come from your mouth. For as a man thinks so is he! The words you speak create life and hope or they bring about death, worry and doubt! So continue to trust God and have faith! Faith is the substance of things hoped for and the evidence of the unseen. Believe like never before and get the vision in your spirit! It is worth it, and it is not in vain!

It's time to take it to a new level.

Are you ready? Get ready! Get ready! Get ready! Make a decision and don't get left behind! It's time to change the way that you see yourself! Do you know who you are? I'm here to remind you that you are a child of God. He is the King Most High! There's none greater than Him! You are an heir of salvation! You are an over-comer! You are more than a conqueror! God sees your potential and what you can become. How do you see yourself? It's time to start seeing yourself as God does and not the world. How you see yourself is how you act. It's time to change! Time to talk the talk and walk the walk! It's time to take *you* to a new level! Are you ready? All you have to do is ask! Your Heavenly Father says you have not because you've asked not! Have you asked? Just know that there's nothing that can separate you from the love of God! Make peace with yourself and then make peace with others! Blessings are upon you, so make the change and live life in God's fulfillment. Nothing missing, nothing empty--just love, peace, joy, good health, happiness and abundance! Take it to a new level.

Oh Lord that you would bless me…

Oh Lord that you would Bless me indeed and enlarge my territory. When you ask for your territory to be enlarged and for more blessings, are you really prepared for what you are asking for? God hears your prayers, and when He Blesses you and enlarges your territory sometimes it can seem overwhelming. You may have a specific idea in mind of how you want your territory designed and how you want your blessings to come, but God is in control. Get ready for any and everything! Get ready for life changing events! It may seem as though you're waiting for your breakthrough, but each and everyday the Lord is enlarging your territory. Those who are faithful with little can be trusted with much. Don't get weary in well doing for you will be rewarded. So continue to pray without ceasing and continue to ask for an enlarged territory, for He says to seek and you would find, knock and the doors would be opened and to ask and you would receive!

Have you heard?

Have you heard that what God has done for others, He'll do for you? He'll pick you up when you're down, He'll turn your life all around! He'll be a friend to the friendless. He will never forsake you! Be like Job and serve Him in good times and bad, because like Job, He will give you double for your trouble. Have you heard that He's an on time God Do you know Him for yourself? Have you heard that He's the same yesterday, today and forever more? He Is! Are you? Did you know that it's not Him that leaves us, but it's us that leaves Him? Have you heard of all the miraculous things He's done? What has He done for you? He woke you up this morning and started you on your way. He put food on your table and a roof over your head! He protected you as you slumbered and slept! So much to be thankful for! Have you heard, that whatever you need all you have to do is go to Him in prayer? If you haven't heard and you don't know, there's no need to be discouraged. Stand still and look up. He's always there, and He has just what you need!

Search yourself!

Are you true? True to you and true to others? Remember that the greatest commandment deals with love! Love your neighbor as you love yourself. Then do unto others as you would have them do unto you. Are your actions pleasing to the Lord? As you examine yourself and your motives, do you like what you see? Your Heavenly Father says that you will reap what you sow. What are you sowing? Just as God will get others for how they treat you, He'll get you for how you treat them. Search yourself and realize that it's important to keep growing. It's not as important where you've been, but where you're going and what you will become. God knows your potential and it's greater than what you see for yourself. Your better days are still before you! Embrace today with truth and love and let God's light shine upon you! Think about what he's brought you through. Search yourself! He says to come to Him like a child and humble yourself. As you elevate God and stop elevating yourself you will see His glory upon you. We must all examine ourselves! For through the examination our will can be released to God's will and God's way! Be true to you and watch what God will do just for you. Search yourself!

The time has come.

It's time! It's time to get your life in order. God said, "If my people who are called by my name would humble themselves and turn from their ways He would save." He's calling you but will you answer the call? Often times people are placed in your life to see if you will pass a test. God wants more for you but He needs to know that you can handle it! Whatever your struggle, give it over to God, He wants to take you to the next level. Will you let Him? It's time to stop just thinking about yourself because your test deals with your reaction--your response. Your Heavenly Father said, "For the least you've done unto them you've done unto me." It's time to step up your game and learn all the right rules! Life isn't about the rules you make, but the rules He did create. It's time to pass the test and receive God's best. He will give you the strength and He will lead you on. Trust Him. The time has come.

He will do above and beyond!

Just ask, don't waiver, don't doubt, just believe! None are perfect among us here on earth, but we must strive to be better than we are. Though we fall we must get up, we must still rise! God said to seek and you would find, believe and you would receive, to knock and the doors would be opened. Know with Jesus on your side you can't lose. He will go above and beyond, just ask and just do what He wants you to do! If God leads you to a place, He will give you what you need, you will succeed! God wants to show up and show out, He shares His glory with no man! Give your situation and give yourself over to God and watch what He'll do for you. He will provide abundantly, exceedingly more than you could ever ask, hope, dream or imagine. Lay it on the altar, He wants to see you through. He can do *all* things! Today go to Him and ask whatever it is you so desire! He will go above and beyond!

Do you have it?

How have you gotten to the place you are in life? We've come this far by faith, leaning on the Lord and trusting in His word. Faith is the substance of things hoped for and the evidence of the unseen. It is impossible to please God without it. What do you believe? Who do you believe? While driving to work in your car you had the faith that you would reach your destination right? When you woke up this morning and planted your feet on the floor, you believed you could walk right? We must trust God and keep our focus on Him! God says to put your trust in no man for he will deceive you, but to put your hope and trust in Him! You can do all things through Him which strengthens you. Don't be sad when things haven't gone as you had planned, just turn it over to God and let Him have His way! It will be greater than you imagined! It's time to recharge and release your faith. Greatness is here! Do you hear it? Faith!

He sees the best in you!

God looks beyond our faults. He looks beyond our imperfections and loves us in spite of them. God knows who you are and what you can become. God wants us to surrender to Him and let Him have His way! He can take a nobody and turn them into somebody. The issues and insecurities, the sin and the shame, the worry and worthlessness is what He can and will take away. He sees the best in you. Go to God in prayer, it's about you and Him. Ask Him for forgiveness and repent, because through asking, being sincere and coming forth in truth you can be set free--free from the bondage that holds you down and holds you back. No matter what you've done, God sees the best in you! Yesterday is gone, tomorrow is not here, but today is now! Live in the present and in God's presence! Today it's time to press in and press on and allow God to move you on! He knows all! Remember He sees the best in you!

Others want what you have.

What will they endure? It's funny how people think they know you, but they don't know the whole story! God called and created you to be who you are, so be happy and be proud. It's your journey that's brought you to where you are today! When they scandalize your name, forgive them for they know not what they do. When they turn their backs on you and look at you in shame, forgive them, for they know not what they do. When they plot and take your good to mean evil, forgive them! Forgive them as often as you can. Forgive them even if they don't ask! You will be rewarded by your Heavenly Father! They don't know the whole story. No one knows your struggles or what it took to get to where you are. That's okay because like a seed that's been planted, watered, rooted up, and grounded, you will rise! Rise to the greatness of God's purpose for your life. Trust God, He knows the whole story! Get ready, the best hasn't even begun! It's true, others want what you have.

Do you know what I know?

      The Lord is great and mighty in battle! Worthy to be praised! He is alpha and omega, the beginning and the end! He heals the sick, feeds the poor, gives shelter to the homeless, yes He's even a friend to the friendless. He's everything you need when you need Him. Did you know He will never leave or forsake you! He's an on-time God! There's none like Him! No one can compare! He's a sovereign God and He reigns! Does he reign in your life? What has your focus these days? Is your mind stayed on Him? If not refocus and let Him have His way. When we lose focus and get caught up in the events of the world, we lose sight of Him and we start to stumble in our lives. Yes trials and tribulations come, but only to make us stronger. Let's face it, God wants you to see Him as your source and to look to Him. He says, "Look up to the hills from whence cometh your help, your help comes from me!" Let Him reign, let Him have His way. He's worthy! Do you know what I know? If so, spread the word!

Got me going in circles!

What am I to do? What has you going in circles and what will you do? Seek you first the kingdom of Heaven and all will be added unto you. Remember in all thy getting though to get an understanding. Understanding allows you to move out of the rut of running around in circles. Constantly going in circles makes you dizzy, confused and perplexed or discombobulated. Who can sustain this for long periods of time? No one! Put your hope and trust in God and know that He is bringing you through, He is taking you over! No longer do you have to worry just let go and let God! Stop where you are right now, and look up and thank God for This is the day that He has made, so rejoice! Take your focus off going in circles and put your focus on the Lord! Get an understanding deep rooted within and know that He is God and that all things work together for the good of those that love the Him! Time to get off the merry-go-'round.

Do you BLOG?

BLOG =

<u>B</u>lame others when things don't go as you had planned?

<u>L</u>ie about the simple things that don't matter?

<u>O</u>pportunist behavior--not caring how or what you have to do to get yours?

<u>G</u>oing and playing by your own rules or using others?

Examine yourself! We have all fallen short for none are perfect! Let him who is without sin cast the first stone! Just because we aren't perfect doesn't give us an excuse to do what we want to do at any cost. It's time to go back to the basics. Go back to the mail.

MAIL =

<u>M</u>ake allowances for others, for they have been made for you.

<u>A</u>ccept others, for we are all unique.

<u>I</u>ndulge in finding ways to help one another.

<u>L</u>ove Unconditionally as Christ loves you.

When we slow down and examine ourselves are we truly pleased with what we see? Examine yourself! For God so loved the world, that He gave His only begotten son. What will you give? Just trust God! We can do it. We can do all things through Him which strengthens us.

Let it go!

The time has come! Forgetting what lies behind and pressing toward the higher mark. Let it go! Let go of that which no longer serves you and means you no good. When we let it go and get rid of all the old baggage that we've hung on to for so long then we have made room to receive. God said that He would open a window and pour out blessings that you wouldn't have room to receive them all. The time has come so clean up your house, clean up your thoughts and get rid of that baggage. It's time for a new and better you! Holding on causes your life to be stagnant when time itself is constant. It's time to grow by letting go. How long will you wait and how long will you hold on? Let it go! As you let it go, you are releasing the blessings of God in your life! The longer you keep it, the longer it takes for you to reach your destiny! God wants His best for you! Do you want it? Well let go and let God!

What's your worth?

Don't get too mighty! Sure I know you are a child of the King Most High. You are made in His image. God said, "The least of you shall the greatest and the last shall be first!" What's your worth? First humble yourselves and don't think yourself too high. God has given you the power to get wealth, have good health and to seek wisdom. But in all thy getting, get an understanding. Where is your humility? Do you serve others or are you constantly being the one served? Remember that greater is He that is in you than he that is in the world. As we humble ourselves and look out for others and fulfill a need, God sees that you are a good and faithful servant. Serving others, doing good deeds, praying the will of God, loving one another, seeking and believing in your Heavenly Father pleases Him most. Your reward will be great, but you must choose what's more important, praise in man's sight or the glory of God? So I say what's your worth? Sure, as a man thinketh so is He! But as you think and as you see yourself, see yourself through Gods eyes and be what He wants you to be! Your worth comes from the Lord!

When God has a plan.

Don't you know that when God has a plan it takes precedence over all other plans? Be patient and wait on the Lord! God has a plan for your life and there's isn't anything that man can do about it. Step aside and let Him have His way, for a righteous man's steps are ordered by the Lord. You see when God has a plan then that means He's for you. God for you is more than the world against you. God's plan makes a provision for you. God's plan makes a way out of no way. God's plan gives you favor and places you at the right place and at the right time. God's plan for your life puts you in His will. Are you willing? Remembering where He brought you from and how He's delivered you--just know that it's all part of His plan. When the enemy comes to attack you and take what's yours, stand strong and wait on the Lord. He will renew your strength, there will be no strongholds that can hold you down. Like Saul who was elevated to a king given his situation, Esther with all her beauty became a queen and saved her people, Ruth and her favor. Joseph and his life being spared, given favor and restoration for all that was lost. When God has a plan nothing or no one can stop Him. Stand still and be of good courage because God has a plan for you.

It's time to take off the gloves.

It's Time to take off the gloves and go back to the basics! Time to go back in training mode. When you're training for that big race or event, you ask your trainer what you should and shouldn't do. You want to make sure that you're doing everything right so that the outcome will turn out pleasing. In going through your daily activities of life, who do you ask? Do you strike out on your own and just assume that you're doing what's right? Well, I'm here to tell you, it's time to Ask! Ask your Heavenly Father, if the words of your mouth and the meditation of your heart are acceptable unto the Him? Are you doing what He wants? Take the time to study and show yourself approved unto God. Ask the Lord daily what to do in every aspect of your life. Seek Him and His opinion first and I guarantee that you will be prepared for everything you need in life to survive and conquer. You serve an awesome God who reigns from Heaven above! Look at His position and who He is! You have the greatest resource to guide you through life so use it. With God you can't lose, so stick to the basics! Asking God always! Take off the gloves and get busy with God.

Don't worry, be happy!

God has not given you a spirit of fear, but one of peace, love, joy and a sound mind. "If you're overwhelmed," He says. "Come to me all who are heavy laden and burdened and I will give you rest." If you worry, why pray? And if you pray, why worry? It's time to turn it all over to your Heavenly Father. Surrender it all. If you call on Jesus, all things are possible. It's time to realize that when you let God have control, you do just that! Let go and let God! Don't you know that worry is just fear? False evidence appearing real! Trust in God He will never forsake you! You must have faith, for it is impossible to please God without it. So the next time you're tempted to worry or fret and are bogged down with all the cares of your life, your family, your friends and the world, turn it over to God and get your rest. Acknowledge that your God is bigger than any problem! He can heal, deliver, transform, renew and restore! He can do everything but fail. So today, I say don't worry! Be happy *now!*

Do you remember or did you forget?

In the name of Jesus, you have the victory! In the name of Jesus Satan has to flee. Bind everything that hinders you and is not of God and release everything that is, such as love, mercy, grace, good health, prosperity and salvation. You get the point. It's time to exercise the authority that God has given you. It's time to speak things that be not as though they were. Speak victory, speak blessings over your life daily. Rise to the occasion and realize that you are more than a conqueror. I say, where is your faith? The Lord says that if you have faith the size of a mustard seed that you can move mountains. What mountains are in your life? What's holding you back? Do you remember or did you forget? It's time to have your strength renewed. It's time to mount up like wings on eagles. It's time to soar! God has not forgot about you, so don't forget about Him! Do you remember or did you forget all the great things He's done for you and others? Always remember and never forget, He's got the whole world in His hands!

What do you do?

What do you do when you've done all you can? Do you continue trying or do you reach for God's Heavenly hands? Do you seek out man? Well I'm here to remind you that with God you stand, because with Him whatever it is you surely can. God can do everything but fail. He will give you an amazing story to tell. He's always there, all you have to do is call on Jesus, His Holy name. God never changes, He's always the same. Once again, just a reminder, it's time out for playing games. Don't seek fortune and fame, because when that's all you have, there will be no one to blame. What do you do when a decision has to be made? Call on your Heavenly Father to come to your aide. No one is greater than He! Knowledge is power and wisdom is key. It's time for the world to see and believe. Tell them what He's done for you. Remind them about His love, grace and mercy. So when you don't know what to do, lift up your hands and begin giving thanks. As you elevate the Lord, your issues become smaller and the guidance you need is written out in front of you. Seek God first and He will do the rest.

God wants more for you!

Only the chosen will survive. You will survive when you pray and cease not. Hold on to God's unchanging hand. God wants more for you, but the question is do you? God wants you happy, satisfied, prosperous and healthy. I know it may seem at times that He's not coming exactly when you want Him, but God has His own time. He's an on- time God, so never forget it! He knows when, how and where He's gonna do it. He just wants to know that you can handle it and that you will do His will. You see it isn't by chance that you're reading this message. He wants to have your undivided attention and He wants to know that you choose Him! Remember everything good and perfect comes from Him. So be faithful, love one another, put your hope and trust in God and learn to give. Give and it shall be given back unto you. God wants more for you!

Do you remember the time?

Do you remember when you felt so alone? When it seemed that everything was an uphill journey and a no-win battle? When you didn't know what you would do or if you would even make it through? Who came to the rescue? Who turned your gray skies blue? Who gave you sunshine on those cloudy days? Who made a way out of no way? Nobody but Jesus! He's your friend, and He's your confidant. Never leaving or forsaking you. Trust in Him with all your heart, mind, body and spirit and lean not to your own understanding. Do you remember who woke you up this morning and who started you on your way? Nobody but the Lord! So next time when you're feeling low and you just don't know, remember that God is there and He always has been! Look around and remember where He's brought you from and what He's brought you through and know that He'll never forget about you! So always remember Him!

Stop! Selah! Listen! Focus!

Proceed! Stop right now what you're doing. Selah-Take a moment to pause and reflect. Listen to what your inner man is saying. Focus on the task at hand that God is giving you. Proceed to do what the Lord has asked of you. In this busy world that we live in excuses seem to be oh so common. Whether we're making them up and telling others or keeping them to ourselves to stop us from taking the necessary steps we should take for our good and the good of others. If we're not careful we miss out on the very thing that God has for us. It is about being at the right place and at the right time. You see our lives are purposed and it is to etify the Lord. As we stop making excuses and surrender ourselves to the true will of God then we are where He wants us to be. Today reach out and do the right thing. Stop being so busy for even yourself. Idle hands create the devil's work, but busy bodies often miss doing the deeds of the Lord. What profits a man to gain the world yet lose his soul? Nothing! It's time to be about the right kind of business. God's business! So stop! Selah! Listen! Focus! Proceed!

Make things happen.

Be a visionary and make things happen! Don't just sit back and let things happen. Yes, we are to be still and know that He is God. He is the Great I Am! Remember He said to knock and the door shall be opened, Seek and we would find, believe and receive. You see, God helps those that help themselves. We are to be diligent daily in praying and seeking God. As we set our sights on the Lord and doing His will, He will birth a vision , a desire, a dream inside of us that He wants us to fulfill. God has a plan for your life. Jesus came so that we could have life and live more abundantly. He sought us! When is the last time you went to God just to fellowship, commune and give thanks without asking for something? Do it today! Make it Happen! Acknowledge the Lord in every aspect of your life and watch how your life will change. Think about it, are you ready to make things happen or continue to let them happen? What is God leading you to do? Do it! It's time to make things happen!

It's not about you!

That's right, it's not about you. Not your will but God's will, will be done! It's about Gods plan and His purpose for your life. Oh too often we get caught up in thinking it's about us and doing our own thing. Just as you think it's about you, God steps in to provide you with the distinct clarity that He is our Heavenly Father and He has the final word! His word is truth and everlasting, it never changes. His word you can trust, believe, and depend. It's not about you! As you realize that it's more about God and serving Him, you learn to break down and let it go. You surrender! All things are to be done to the glory of God. Your prayers will be heard and answered as you delight yourself in the Lord, He will fulfill your desires. Make the Lord the light of your life and He will be a light unto your path. Let not your heart be troubled! As you make it about Him, it will be about you!

Make it plain!

What are you in need of? God says to write the vision down, make it plain and clear, be specific on what you need, so that when He fulfills it and others read what He has done, they can go and tell of His greatness. Remember to make your requests known unto God, and that though the vision may tarry, your request delayed, wait for it! For it is yet at an appointed time. God is always on time and He knows what we need, just when we need it most. Since God shares His glory with no man, He wants to make sure He's getting the credit. God said He would supply all your needs, not just some of them! So as you're waiting for the vision to manifest, go about your day counting it as joy! We are to be happy and of a good spirit. Make it plain to see that you're not worried! Worry is the will of the adversary! So talk to Jesus and take some time to write out your requests. Don't be afraid to communicate, for through communication great things can be accomplished! Keep it simple, and if you don't know what you need, then ask God! Be faithful.

What rules you?

Is it your job? Is it your friends? Your circumstances? Finances? Significant other? Spouse? Self defeating mentality that's afraid of success? Loneliness? Depression? Negative thoughts? Fear? What rules you? Think about it! God says to cast your cares upon Him, for He cares for you! Nothing is too big or too small for Him to handle! He can do everything but fail! It's time to lay those things on the altar that rule you! It's time to move to the next level of your life. Nothing and no one is greater than God! He should be ruler of your life! He reigns and Jesus came. Came to take away the sin, the worry and the doubt! Came so you could have everlasting life. Don't waste it! No more fear of anything in your life, because fear is false evidence appearing real! With God you have what you need! What profits a man to gain the world and lose His soul? So next time it seems as though something is ruling you, and has you overly consumed, just say *Bless the Lord O My Soul and all that is within me,* then remember and forget not all His benefits and let Him rule in your life.

It's another day's journey.

Are you glad about it? Well, this is the day that the Lord has made so let us rejoice and be glad about it! Yes, today is a new beginning and a chance to be better than yesterday. Yesterday is gone, never to return again, but today is now and tomorrow isn't promised to come. Make the most of where you are right now in the present and don't let good things pass you by. Relax and stop over analyzing and learn to go with the flow. Let the Lord lead you throughout your journey today and every day. He's ready for the asking. Let Him be your tour guide and listen closely and carefully to all He tells you. You don't want to miss out on a thing! As you settle in your mind what God is showing you, doing for you and doing through you, then the wisdom of the Lord will truly be in you! Rejoice in hope, be patient in affliction, and persistent in prayer! You can make it! So smile. It is another day's journey. Are you ready for it?

Watch out!

As we go through our daily lives we must learn to wait as well as watch! For they that wait upon the Lord He shall renew their strength. We must watch for the signs that the Lord is giving us. If we wait and watch a little longer things will be revealed. Don't get weary in well doing and don't worry when you make a mistake for God is with you and He can fix and make everything all right. Remember that nothing is too hard for your God! Wait and watch others, for if you wait and watch long enough a person's motives will be revealed. Think about yourself, are you shedding old skin? What do others see and how do you treat them, how are you perceived? None of us are perfect and we all fall short sometimes. Do you judge me based on others? Do others judge you based on others? Learn to let go and to let God. Realize you are responsible for your actions, so wait and watch and be the best that you know how to be! God is on your side, so be encouraged no matter what the situation. Live. Love. Let go and watch out!

Time to be ye steadfast.

It is truly time to abound in the word of the Lord! Do you know what the word says about your situation? It's time to have faith. Faith the size of a mustard seed so that you can move mountains. It's time to Love. Did you know that love conquers all? Love is the greatest gift of them all and God's love is unconditional. Is yours? Seek Him, He won't let you down! Do you know what He says about loneliness? He said lo I will be with you always. He promises never to leave you or forsake you. Do you know what He says about doubt and fear? He says to "doubt not in your heart and believe. To fear not for I am with you, be not dismayed for I am your God, I will strengthen you, I will help you, I will uphold you with my righteous right hand!" So as you get the word within and you truly start to realize, who you are and whose you are in Christ then you are awakened to the victory of abundance and life everlasting! Be ye steadfast and unmoved by the situation and circumstances. Get in your word and trust your Heavenly Father! He has the answers to all your questions and He can make a way out of no way! Be encouraged and seek ye first the kingdom of Heaven and watch all be added unto you, according to His riches and His glory in Heaven.

Believe!

It's time again! Remember when we were kids and it was so easy to believe? Whatever your parents told you they'd do, you believed. If they said it, chances are that's the way it would be. We even believed in fairy tales and make believe. We believed in ourselves and we believed in each other! It's time to believe in your Heavenly Father. Believe in His word. If God says it, so it shall be! We must not lose the faith and fill our hearts with doubt and disbelief. We must believe! Jesus said that if you can believe, all things are possible to those that do truly believe! God so loved the world that He gave His only begotten son so whoever believeth shall not perish but have everlasting life! Let not your heart be troubled He says but believe in Him. Believe and He will do great works in you and through you. Be not faithless but believe. God has given you the power to attain what you want in life, but you must believe! Delight yourself in Him and He will give you the desires of your heart. The only way to get there is to believe! Do you believe? If not, it's time again to believe and let God's glory and goodness manifest in your life!

Acceptable or not?

What are the words you're speaking? How is your behavior? Examine yourself! Keeping it real with yourself, acceptable or not? Daily when you rise do you give thanks unto the Lord, for being blessed to see another day? There are many that retired to rest last night, never to rise again to Earthly life. You're Blessed! He says study to show yourself approved unto me, your God! It's about pleasing Him! Have you asked Him lately, *Lord, May the words of my mouth and the meditation of my heart be acceptable unto you O God?* He says to present your bodies as a living sacrifice, holy and acceptable. Do you constantly build up only to tear down? Is it self destruction or destruction of others? Unacceptable! Your Heavenly Father says that life and death are in the power of the tongue. Speak blessings over your life and the life of others. Now *that's* acceptable! God says to love your neighbor as you love yourself. Acceptable! Treat others as you would have them treat you! Acceptable! Seek God to lead, guide and direct your path. Remember a righteous man's steps are ordered by the Lord! Today take some time to look at the man in mirror, and examine him. Is He acceptable or not?

STAND!

When you've done all you can do, just stand! You can call upon the Lord, for He cares for you! Time out for looking at the situation and the circumstances but trusting God to see you through. He knows what's best for you. When it seems that it's an uphill battle and you've given all you can, just stand! Your Heavenly Father says to put your trust in no man, for he will deceive you. Trust in the Lord, for He will never leave, deceive or forsake. He is with you always! To stand, you must have faith. Believe in difficult times when it seems impossible and know that God is in control of your life. Pray and cease not and just know that the end result means victory if you hold on to God's unchanging word! He is the same yesterday, today and forever more. So stand and trust God, things will work out! All things work together for the good of those that love the Lord! Stand! It's sometimes difficult, but worth it and you won't regret it! Stand!

You have the power!

Release the fear and exercise your authority! God does not give you the spirit of fear, but of peace, love, joy and a sound mind! God has given you the authority to have dominion! Too many times when the enemy comes to attack us we find ourselves worrying, crying and giving in to the situation. It's time that you start fighting back! It's time that you realize who you are and who you belong to! You are an heir of salvation, purchased by God! You have the victory. God chose you long ago! Because you are a child of the King Most High, you have all the benefits that come with that. In those times of discouragement and despair remember to look up to the hills, from whence cometh your help! Your help comes from the Lord, which made Heaven and earth. He will not suffer your foot to be moved, He never slumbers nor sleeps. Call on Jesus, with Him nothing is impossible, but all thing are possible! As long as you've got the Lord, the enemy can't prevail! Speak things that be not as though they were! You have the authority so speak it and speak up!

What's going on?

Why do you doubt? Why are you of little faith? Think back to a difficult time in your life when God brought you through. He delivered you, spared you and saved you. You are here today and for a purpose! Could have been me or it could have been you, but it is someone who is going through. Going through something that they just don't know what to do, but when you call of Jesus, all things are possible! Don't give up and don't give in! Let your praise unto God be automatic. Just do it. Work on it! Remember with God on your side, things will work out fine! How can you lose, if it's the name Jesus that you use? You can't! What's going on? Are you lonely, broken-hearted or in despair? Are you broke, busted and disgusted? Have you lost your job or just lost your way? There's no need to worry! God has you in the palm of hand. No weapon formed against you will prosper! God favors you! Look to God! Take it in stride and know that no matter what the situation, the best is yet come! Hold on and give it to God, no matter what's going on!

Check Yourself!

Don't wreck yourself! What are the messages that you send out daily to the people you interact with? You must remember that a tongue can be as sharp as a two-edged sword, cutting deep. Learn to watch your words and guard your tongue. Life and death are in the power of the tongue. You say you didn't mean to say it or do it and that you were in a bad mood or things didn't go your way. That's no excuse! Check yourself before you wreck yourself and relationships that you deem important in your life. Of course you can be forgiven. God forgives but man is not always so kind! We are responsible for our own actions! Trust God and ask Him to help you where you fall short. We all need His help, for we can't make it without Him. With Him we are made whole and our actions reflect who He is in our lives. God has *all* the answers so seek Him. If you let God be the captain of your ship, you can't wreck, it's smooth sailing! Although the waves may come, you will know how to respond and not react! Check yourself and let God lead you!

You can make it!

You are destined for greatness! Remember that you can do all things through Christ which strengthens you! Your help comes from the Lord! Trials and tribulations come only to make us stronger. He promised never to leave or forsake us! What are you in need of today? Is it a friend? Is it finances? A job? A little joy? Love? Laughter? Whatever it is, know that when you call on Jesus all things are possible! He says you have not because you've asked not! You can make it through whatever you're going through and you can have whatever you're in need of. Ask and believe and doubt not! It's time to speak things as though they were! You are destined for greatness so speak it and act like it! It's time to realize who you are in Christ! You can and you will make it!

Do you worry?

Why worry? It's time to turn everything over to your Heavenly Father! Man should always pray. Pray without ceasing! God says not to worry about anything! Don't worry about everyday life, whether you have enough food to eat, what to wear, your health, your relationships, your job or your finances. When will you realize that life is more than food, material things, wealth, etc. you can truly appreciate life and the simple things. Birds are singing, happy and flying about. They don't worry about a thing. God takes care of them and He values you more! What will He do for you? Learn to be free as a bird. Look at how the flowers grow and blossom. They don't worry. They weather the storm and keep on growing for all the world to see their beauty. Be like a flower, keep growing and let your inner beauty come forth. Never let them see you down. Seek the Kingdom of God first and He will give you what you need. Remember: don't worry, but believe in God! Trust Him! Worry is wrong thinking, opportunities lost, remembering only negative, reaching and not believing, yielding to the situation and circumstances! Don't worry! Have faith!

Isn't he wonderful?

Isn't He wonderful! Isn't He amazing? Isn't He worthy! Oh yes He is! The Lord is the Great I Am and there's none like Him! Just know that No one can do you
like the Lord! Whatever you're facing or going through have the confidence that God never calls you to do something without enabling and equipping you! Let not your heart be troubled, He is with you always. In times of adversity,
disappointment and discouragement have the Faith in knowing that He will bring you through! He's an on-time God! Think back to where He's brought you from and look ahead to where He wants to take you! Isn't He wonderful! Isn't He amazing! Just Let Him know that He is worthy! So take the time to lift Him up so that others will be drawn unto Him. Remember that when the praises go up, that the blessings will surely come down!

Who's in control?

I just wanna know. Are you Like a puppet on a string, moving about turning and twisting, bending and bowing? Someone is in control. Is it the daily stresses of the job? The uncertainty of what tomorrow will bring? Is it society or is it your spouse? Your family or your friends? Who's in control? Do you have a puppet master? Think long and hard before responding. Who's in control? I say it is time to let God have control of you! Let him lead, guide and direct you. A righteous man's steps are ordered by the Lord. Seek God and choose Him, for He chose you a very long time ago. Let Him have His way! God offers you peace, protection and His promises! The life you live will let others know if your light is brightly shining or dimly lit. It's time to take center stage, will the lights go up? I ask, who's in control?

Today is going to be a great day!

Today realize that there are so many wonderful people in your life. Today be more thankful. Today find beauty in the simple things. Today expect good news. Today let your light shine. Everything truly begins with today! Start today for it is the beginning of the rest of your life. It's up to you to live a meaningful and fulfilled life. It's time to do you! Just do what makes you happy! It doesn't matter what others say and what others think, do what you like and what's pleasing to the Lord. Be sure that whatever it is, that it's for the good of all and the harm of none. You know what you want and what you need. Is it status quo? Live to the fullest! Today is your day!

Don't stop, keep on going!

Don't stop, keep on going! Don't stop, keep on growing! Don't stop, Keep on loving! Don't stop, Keep on praying. Don't stop, keep on believing! Though the road gets rough and the going gets tough hold on! The change
you've been waiting for is here! Be ye not conformed of this world. Trust in the Lord your God with All your heart, your mind, your spirit and your soul! Lean not to your own understanding! God is working it out! Just know that God
never calls you to do something without enabling you. So when He calls you can rest assured that He's made it possible for you to do it! God knows what you are capable of! It's time you start seeing yourself as God does! So I say to you, don't stop, keep on because your latter days will be greater. The best is yet to come! Don't stop, keep on going.

You really have the victory!

Rejoice for you have the victory! Don't wait until you see things manifested in the natural, start shouting, rejoicing, smiling and praising God now! Praise Him in advance! When you're happy and you' know it clap your hands, stomp your feet, shout for joy! When you're secure in the Lord, then you're not afraid to show it! Whatever the battle, God says it's not yours, but it's His! Victory and honor come from God alone! Remember that He shares His glory with no man! Let God be your refuge and your rock, your enemy won't be able to reach you. Please trust in God at all times and pour your heart out to him. He is your refuge! If the need is a job, a mate, a doctor, a lawyer, a friend, a parent, an opportunity, someone to listen, He's always there! When you call on Jesus never forget that all things are possible! It's time to work on pleasing God, for whatever you need. He will supply! Start speaking victory over your life!

No matter where you are in life!

No matter where you are in this world or where you are in life, stop and say, "Today is going to be a great day!" This is the day that the Lord has made, let us rejoice and be glad in it! Expect great things and doubt not. For if you have the faith the size of a mustard seed you can move mountains! Remember God for you is more than the world against you! He is the same yesterday, today and forever more! Expect great things! He gives grace, mercy, salvation and love! Have you forgotten that He's an on-time God! Expect great things! He created Heaven and Earth and all there within! He created light out of darkness. Can He not do what you need? Do you know what

His promises are for your life? If not it's time to find out! He's not a man that He should lie! If God said it, so it shall be! Expect great things and speak it! All things are possible but you must believe! No matter where you are in life, trust God!

You are where you're supposed to be.

You are where you're supposed to be! Make a choice! Choose life, joy and celebrate! Or choose lack of motivation, self pity, loneliness and complaining! You're where you're supposed to be! Trials and tribulations come only to make us stronger! No matter where you are today in life, choose to celebrate and thank God! Remember there's always someone who is worse off than you. We may not be comfortable in certain situations but pray your way through! The prayer of a righteous man availeth much! God knows all and sees all! He knows what you're thinking and when you're thinking it! So I say enjoy the journey that you are on and learn! Celebrate, rejoice, live and be thankful and grateful to God! Praise gets you through what you're going through.

On Your Mark!

On your mark! Get ready! Get set! Go! Are you ready for the race? Well whether you're ready or not the race is going on! But will you? There's still time and it's never too late! Start now training your body, your mind, your heart and your spirit. Surround yourself w/ believers and get in the Holy word! Know what Gods word says about your situation and speak those things that be not as though they were! Guard your thoughts and surround yourself with positive people! You have everything inside of you to run and win this race! On your mark, get ready, get set…Go!!!

Knock, knock!

If anyone hears me will you let me in? Sometimes we can be closed off and in our own worlds we miss that which is at our own front door. When opportunity comes knocking will you hear it? Will you see it? Will you feel it? Will you know it? How will you know? Go to God and ask Him! He wants to partner with you in every aspect of your life! He says No good thing will I with hold from you! Depend on Him, lean not to your own understanding and you will know! God can open doors that no man can close and he can shut doors that no man can open! With God on your side things *will* work out! Open the door!

Are you driving?

Are you driving or are in the passenger's seat? Who's driving you and what drives you? It's time to move over if you're in the passenger's seat or get up front if you're riding in the back! Stop waiting! Take action and get in the driver's seat and let the Lord navigate you! The
time is now, So fill up, clean up, pack up and get moving! God wants to take you to great places. He wants nothing but the best for you! Get in the driver's seat and let Him Navigate the way! It's time to truly trust Him! Get ready for the ride and know that nothing can stop you but you!

Amazing grace!

Oh yes it is! We must realize that God's grace is sufficient for us! His love, grace and mercy endureth to all generations! When you're feeling down and all alone look up and give thanks because God is there. When you're feeling on top of the world and all is going right, look up and give thanks! God is there! He says, "I will be with you always!" You're never alone! God is so amazing, don't forget about Him, and He won't forget about you!

Do you ever wonder why?

Do you know what makes you unique? Are you ready to live to the fullest? Do you know how to overcome? Are you a survivor? Do you treat others how you want to be treated? Do you keep your word? Can you be counted on? Study to show yourself approved unto God! If others were asked these same questions about you what would they say? When you know who you are in Christ, then you can live to the fullest! You are made in God's image, so make sure the daily image you're portraying is one that God would be proud of! We all fall short! If at first you don't succeed, don't stop. Keep trying!

Never forget!

Never forget about God's Grace and His Mercy! Never forget how He gave His only begotten Son, so that we could have life. Never forget that Christ died on the cross so that we could have eternal life. Don't forget who woke you up this morning and started you on your way. Never forget that weeping may endure for a night, but joy comes in the morning. Never forget that with every ending, that there is a new beginning. Never forget that God loves you and He will see you through whatever you're going through. Never forget, He said to cast your cares on Him for He cares for you. Don't forget that He said to seek Him First, seek the Kingdom of Heaven and All else will be added unto you. God is good and faith endures to all generations. Bless His name for He is worthy. So the next time you're having a hard time, remember that He is the Author and the Finisher of your life. He has All power and He has already worked things out in your situation, so lean not to your own understanding, but Trust in the Lord! Take time to remember!

Time to shine!

No man knows the second, minute, hour or day when He shall appear again! No one can predict the last breath that he or she will take! Sometimes you only get one chance, so what will you do with yours? Shine as bright as you can and let your light lead someone! Remember to love your God with all your heart mind and soul and to love your neighbor as you love yourself! People helping people! Shine!

Get in the zone!

It's time to focus on what matters most to you! Let not your heart be troubled for God is with you always! It's time to get out the land of regret and move forward. The choice is yours! Get in the zone and focus on what you want. Believe it, believe in yourself and most importantly believe in God. All things are possible to those that believe! It's closer than you think, so get in the zone!

Release the knots and renew your mind!

It's time to reach for the ultimate experience. You can make it through anything! Exit from that old mind set of doing things and strive to do and be the very best you can be. Don't half do anything! Despite your setbacks release the knots and set the traps to stop doubt, lack, sickness, loneliness or whatever holds you back. Get the vision clear in your mind and wait for it. It is yet for an appointed time. Release the knots and let God go to work! He can create a new work in you. The ultimate experience: joy, peace, love, happiness and abundance--all that's good. Release the knots and renew your mind.

Today is a new beginning, so embrace this moment with celebration!

Making it to see another day, the ability to continue to have breathe, knowing that your future is bright! God said that He is with us always! Trials and tribulations strengthen us to continue to run this race. God has not given up on you, so never give up on yourself! Hold your head high, smile, and be thankful for the things you have and stop reflecting on what you don't have! In due time that which God has for you shall be yours! So keep joy alive! Today is a new beginning, so embrace this moment with celebration!

Cherish the moment!

Take some time to cherish the moment, to cherish where you are, to cherish where you've been and to cherish where you are going. Too often in life we get in a hurry and its instant and self gratification that we seek. Realize that there's a purpose and a plan for your life. If you don't take the time to stop and see the beauty around you or to be thankful for all the wonderful things that God has done for you and doing for you, You will miss enjoying the journey and life will pass you by. Cherish the moment and cherish the memories. I understand that everyday may not go exactly as we would have planned, but trust and know that God something special and it's just for you! Greet each day with thankfulness and being grateful and appreciating. Celebrate each day because you are wonderfully made and you are loved, so cherish the day, the time and the people in your life. Have the assurance like never before and know that ALL things work together for the good of those that love the Lord and are called according to His purpose. So I say, Take some time to cherish the now because you can never get it again. Be Blessed!

Showtime! Lights! Camera! Action?

Someone is always watching! We must daily put our best foot forward. Everything we do must be done to the best of our ability. You are the salt of the earth and God says you must let your light shine for all to see! When you're shining bright as the stars you're representing Him! When your light seems as though it's dim, He promises to be a light unto your path! A righteous man's steps are ordered by the Lord and though he stumbles He will not fall! The world is your stage! Who are you performing for? Trust in God and let your light shine! To God be the glory! Lights! Camera! Action!

Divine intervention!

Divine intervention! Sometimes things don't go as we have them planned. So is it divine intervention or is it us getting in the way of ourselves? Regardless nothing happens by coincidence! God knows us better than we know ourselves, yet he continues to love us in spite of! There are times when maybe that job didn't come through or he/she didn't call like they said or the trip you planned never happened, etc. Instead of being sad, Thank God for His divine intervention because you never know what He spared you from! Remember He's all knowing and He knows what's best for you!

Go Deep!

Like those that go deep and drill for oil in the middle of fields or somewhere way offshore. Or those that go deep in mines to search for gold. Go deep within yourself to discover who you are! There's more to you than what meets the eye! You are wonderfully made! The outside fades away, but that which is deep within surfaces for the world to see, will last forever. You are gentle, kind, loving, giving, compassionate and list goes on and on!

You were created in God's image and you are His child, so go deep and let your true value spring up for the world to see! Go deep and let your worth come forth. You are destined for greatness! Will you discover it? Time to go deep!

We all wonder!

Sometimes we wonder *how did I get here? How have I made it?* How? We've come this far by faith, leaning on the Lord! God says I am with you always and I will never leave or forsake you! So don't stop now! When we trust in the Lord we have perfect peace and everlasting strength! So if you've been feeling a little weak lately, just go to God in prayer! He's the same yesterday, today and will be always! Are you the same? Have you spent time with Him lately? Well there's no need to wonder anymore, it's time to realize and recognize that it is He who has made us and not we ourselves! Give God the glory and don't wonder!

God has the final say so!

Do you know that He's all knowing and that He has all power? He is the Great I Am! It's time to let go of the painful thoughts of the past and live to the fullest! He loves you more than you love yourself! He loves you in spite of and not because of! The reward is great so trust Him! He can and will make a way out of no way! Don't give up the fight! No matter the battle just know that the war was already won! Jesus gave His life! Keep pressing forward and remember, God has the final say so!

Live a life of no regret!

There are things of the past that can't be undone, but don't focus on those things. We have all made mistakes. You must press forward! Anything in your past that's holding you back, turn it over and give it to God! Nothing is too hard for Him! Seek God first daily and ask for guidance. It's never too late for God's help so don't live a life of regret! So hold your head up high and embrace today with God's blessed assurance that all is well! Choose to live a life of no regret!

Time for a temperature check!

Where are you right now? Are you on your destiny path? Are you hot, cold or are you just right? When you're hot you think you've got it all figured out and you feel like you don't need anyone you can make it on your own! Cold life passing you by and you can't seem to get out of a rut, problem after problem. When you're just right you're ready, willing and able to ask for help, make a change and learn all that life is willing to teach you! What's your temperature? We must all embrace change and we must realize that we can't make it on our own! We need God to lead, guide and direct us! To send us the right relationships and to help us make decisions that are pleasing to Him to open doors that no man can close! Seek ye first the kingdom of heaven and all will be added unto you! Make a decision to get your temperature checked and make adjustments to live a life of prosperity and abundance! It's your choice! Time for a temperature check.

New chapter. Next book.

Sometimes you have to turn the page and get to the end of the chapter to begin a new book for a new beginning. It may take awhile to get to the end of page but don't stop, just when you think it'll never end, a new chapter is about to begin! As you let go and continue moving along you realize that it only gets better. So let go and let God, He's not only ready for you to start a new chapter but He's ready to give you a new book! Make up your mind to get done with the page and move on to the next chapter to begin your new book. The more you take time to enjoy reading, the greater the chapters will be and the greater the book will be. It's your life, so enjoy it!

What are you wearing?

Are you wearing your best? Whatever the adversity or obstacle make sure you are wearing your best! Never let them see you sweat! Put on your best face, your best attitude and put your best foot forward! Consider the source, then consider *your* source! God's got you, so trust Him. As long as you have God, wear your best and nothing less! When you wear your best, you're always prepared! What are you wearing?

Process=Smile & the world smiles with you! Frown & the world ignores you!

Do good works & let your light shine, for the brighter it shines, it creates warmth and draws others near. Be positive & believe for the best, for positive actions & words will breed positive results. Watch it spread, for it is contagious. Treat others how you want to be treated! This creates a better you! Process=Smile & the world smiles with you! Frown & the world ignores you!

Keep Believing, keep hoping.

Keep living. Keep giving. Keep smiling. Keep loving. Keep moving. Keep pressing forward! Keep helping one another! Keep being the best that you can be! Keep giving it your all! Keep God as the center of your life and He will be the source of your life! Keep knowing that your God shall supply all your needs! Just keep going! Keep believing. Keep hoping. Keep living.

Stop! Look! Listen!

It's time to slow down, stop, look around you and listen! Take notice in the very things that we take for granted. Opening your eyes this morning, taking another breath, seeing the break of day, the sweet smell of flowers, the sound of your heart beating, the voice of a friend or loved one, the opportunity to say *I love you!* The Lord says take no thought for tomorrow for no one knows what it will bring! Today, take notice! Stop! Look! Listen!

Let not your heart be troubled, God is with you ALWAYS!

The storm is over when you let go and let God. We must never forget that trouble doesn't last always! Whatever the trials or tribulations we must remember that our future is brighter than our past! So exit from the thoughts of situations and circumstances of your life and what you're going through and rejoice and be thankful and grateful. There's someone that would love to trade places with you! Let not your heart be troubled, God is with you always!

Call now!

Call on that inner child deep within and release it! Children are fun, free spirits with love and laughter in their hearts! They have great expectations and they believe in what appears to be the impossible! Their spirits recognize that all things are possible to those that really believe and the know that faith brings about change! They may fall down and they may cry, but they remember the good! So call now on that inner child within you and call on God! Call now!

There's so much going on in the world today!

Can anyone truly hear me? Can someone just speak to my heart? Does anyone really listen anymore? I need a breakthrough! Silence no more by the situations of my daily life but letting go! Releasing that which holds back and hinders! No guarantees in life so start living to the fullest! Laughter in my eyes and joy in my heart; I will worship my Lord and give thanks! Perseverance! We can do it! There's so much going on in the world today, so let God have what's going on in *your* world today!

Do You Know the answers?

Do you ever wonder why? Do you know what makes you unique? Are you ready to live to the fullest? Do you know how to overcome? Are you a survivor? Do you treat others how you want to be treated? Do you keep your word? Can you be counted on? Study to show yourself approved unto God! If others were asked these same questions about you, what would they say? When you know who you are in Christ, then can you live to the fullest! You are made in God's image, so make sure the daily image you're portraying is one that God would be proud of! We all fall short! If at first you don't succeed, don't stop--keep trying! The answers are simple so start loving others as you love yourself. Start having mercy as God has mercy for us. Start knowing that God has *all* the answers, and whatever He says is what matters.

Rejoice and be happy!

Smile and walk with the blessed assurance that God's promises for your life will come to pass! Seek ye first the kingdom of God and All else will be added unto you! Give thanks and know that within you is everything you need! Let downs and disappointments? Stressed and in disarray? No! You are special child of God. You are too anointed to be disappointed and too blessed to be stressed! So press on knowing God is on your side! Rejoice in the Lord and be happy, Watch how your circumstances will start to change for the better. Today count it all as joy. Rejoice and be happy!

Oh how amazing it is to rise and see another day!

I will give thanks for every breath I breathe! I will not let a day end without acknowledging my creator! I will not be afraid of the unknown nor will I fear being alone. I am wonderfully made, made in the image of my God. He will protect me and guide me and lead me on the path to greatness! I can do all things through Christ which strengthens me! I am courageous and I am me! Oh how amazing it is to rise and see another day!

Love, mercy and grace: God's greatest gifts.

He loves us, forgives us, consoles us and blesses us! He's so good! He's good despite our actions! No one and nothing compares to Him! Today think about His greatness and what He's done for you! Have faith in God. You can't go wrong, because with Him you go right! If you've missed your turn, do a U-Turn and try again. All roads to life's happiness, prosperity, abundance and good health begin and end with him! Love, mercy and grace: God's greatest gifts.

Clean house!

Yes, a change in yourself to change your situation! It's time to do things differently. Search yourself! Do you have a vision? Though the vision tarry, wait for it, for it is yet at an appointed time. It's time to clean your thinking! As a man thinketh so is He! Clean up those habits that keep getting you those same results! Let go of that which no longer serves you. A clean house=a better you! Praise be to God!

Driving?

Which lane on the highway do you tend to drive in the most? Are often in the right lane going slow and coasting by? Or are you in the center lane moving with a purpose and passing the slow and cautious? Or are you far left moving too fast, rushing and often out of control? Think about it! It's like life in itself, there are those that move slow and let thing happen, those that move with a purpose and make things happen and those that are too fast and busy that life passes them by! Regardless of which lane you're in or where you are in life, take the time to enjoy the journey and realize how you made it from A to Z. The grace of God! Give thanks and live life!

It's time to take watch!

What are you thinking about constantly? What are the words that are coming from your mouth? We must guard our minds and our tongue! If we wait, the Lord gives us understanding in all things! So His word says to speak things that be not as though they were! A guardsman speaks in a manner of authority and says the things that are appropriate. Not speaking in vain! Do you know that God has given you authority? A guardsman has to focus! Idle minds are not allowed! Are you ready to guard? It's time to take watch.

Life without limitations!

Are you ready to live a life without limitations? God says to choose you this day who will serve. Serve God and have life more abundantly. With God, ALL things are possible to those that believe. Make up your mind to stop viewing the world through a tunnel, but view it with eyes wide open and see all that God created you to be and created you to have. Life with endless possibilities is what He promises. He says that you can do ALL things through Him which strengthens you. He wants to get you out of the mind set of thinking small, of thinking lack, of thinking not good enough, not going to happen, can't, won't and impossible. God created earth and all there within. He created you and He created me. Always remember that you are created for a purpose. Not your will, but God's will, will be done. So I ask again, do you want to live a life without limitations? If so, change your thinking, because it's not the world that places limitations on you, but you yourself! You can and you will, but only if you think and believe that you can and you will. Free yourself, and start Living your life Without Limitations!

Don't let it get you down!

Weeping may endure for a night but joy comes in the morning. Don't let it get you down! God said that He would supply ALL of your needs! ALL is All-Inclusive! Whatever you want and whatever you need, make your request known unto God! Don't give up and don't give in to the circumstances that cause you to doubt and wonder if God is listening and if God really cares! He says cast your cares upon me Dear Child, and I will give you rest, I will renew your strength, I will restore, I am the Author and the Finisher and it aint over until I say it's over. God has the final say so didn't you know? Don't let it get you down. Remember there's double for your trouble and that which satan meant for your bad, God will surely turn it around for your good! With God you just can't lose! I say look up, rejoice, give thanks and count it ALL as joy because God won't let you down, so don't let life's setbacks and disappointments get you down! God is taking you up, so don't let IT get you down!

A year has passed you by.

As time is constant and waits for no one, what are you doing with your time? Are you living life to the fullest and making the most of the time you have? The reality is that here today maybe gone tomorrow! Live today! Your Savior died so you could live! Are you living to the fullest? What are you doing with your time? It's never too late, so start living. Don't let a year pass you by!

It's time to release the fears deep within that cause you to be in bondage!

Whether it's starting over again or letting go. Can you continue moving forward or are you holding on to could of, should of and would of? You have the opportunity to do great things and to be great. Great things on this earth and to be great to others and not just in your mind! Find out what's got you bound and deal with it! You are not alone! God will help you! Go to God in prayer! Prayer changes things! God for you is more than the world against you! Release yourself from fear! You can do anything!

Sweet whispers and a gentle touch.

Just call on the sweet name of Jesus and watch your needs be met. Whatever you're in need of, go to God in prayer. He says to seek and you would find, knock and the doors would be opened, and to believe and you will receive. Sweet whispers and a gentle touch...When it seems that you've done all you can, God is holding you and telling you, yes you can, but you *must* stand. Remember that the race is not given to the swift and that the battle is not yours. Everything belongs to the Lord! Lift your head up high and call on His holy name and watch as things begin to change. Quiet yourself so you can hear His voice, and open your heart so you can feel His touch! You're never alone, for to God you surely belong. His grace allows us to shine and our lives to be defined. Sweet whispers and a gentle touch is what we all need from time to time to feel the power of the great divine.

Let him lead you!

That's right! It's time to relinquish control! Remember a righteous mans steps are ordered by the Lord. Acknowledge Him in all your ways and He will direct your path. Allow God to order your steps every day. With God in control you'll never be left out in the cold. Don't look at the situation and the circumstances or lean to your own understanding, just trust God to do what He said He'd do! Let Him lead you and don't doubt what He tells you! He will never give you more than you can handle and knows just how much you can bare. Don't second guess what the Lord gives you because it will always work out right! You are more than a conqueror! You can't fail! You have what it takes to succeed, to make it to the next level, to be prosperous! You can have it all! God wants only the best for you. So today, get out of your own way and let the Lord lead you!

www.ingramcontent.com/pod-product-compliance
Lightning Source LLC
Chambersburg PA
CBHW031042110426
42740CB00046B/653